READING POWER

European Colonies
in the Americas

Russian Colonies in the Americas

Lewis K. Parker

The Rosen Publishing Group's
PowerKids Press™
New York

Published in 2003 by The Rosen Publishing Group, Inc.
29 East 21st Street, New York, NY 10010

First Edition

Book Design: Erica Clendening

Photo Credits: Cover, pp. 4, 6, 14–15 © North Wind Picture Archives; p. 5 Erica Clendening; p. 8 Library of Congress, Prints and Photographs Division; p. 9 Library of Congress, General Collections; p. 10 (inset) Oregon Historical Society #82934; pp. 10–11, 18 © Hulton/Archive/Getty Images; pp. 11 (inset), 13, 16–17 courtesy Fort Ross; p. 12 © Michael T. Sedman/Corbis; p. 19 © Tom Benoit; p. 21 © Bettmann/Corbis

Library of Congress Cataloging-in-Publication Data

Parker, Lewis K.
Russian colonies in the Americas / Lewis K. Parker.
    v. cm. — (European colonies in the Americas)
Includes bibliographical references and index.
Contents: First voyages — Tragedy and triumph — Settling Alaska — Russian trading — The Russian-American Company — Fort Ross — The end of Fort Ross — Russia and the United States — Selling Alaska.
ISBN 0-8239-6470-1 (library binding)
1. America—Discovery and exploration—Russian—Juvenile literature.
2. Russians—America—History—Juvenile literature. 3. Alaska—Discovery and exploration—Russian—Juvenile literature. 4. Russia—Colonies—America—History—Juvenile literature. [1. America—Discovery and exploration—Russian. 2. Russians—America—History. 3. Alaska—Discovery and exploration—Russian. 4. Russia—Colonies—America. 5. Frontier and pioneer life—Alaska. 6. United States—History—Colonial period, ca. 1600-1775.] I. Title.
E135.R87 P37 2003
979.8'02—dc21

                                            2002000156

Contents

First Voyages

For hundreds of years, only Native Americans lived in what is now Alaska. In 1648, a Russian explorer found a strait, or narrow waterway, between Russia and Alaska. It led to the Pacific Ocean. Russian hunters began to use the strait to find sea otters and seals that lived nearby. They sold the furs of these animals in China for a lot of money.

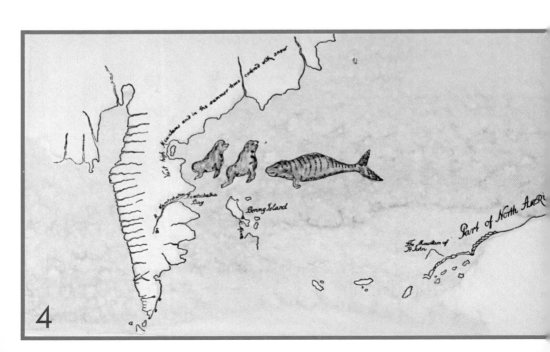

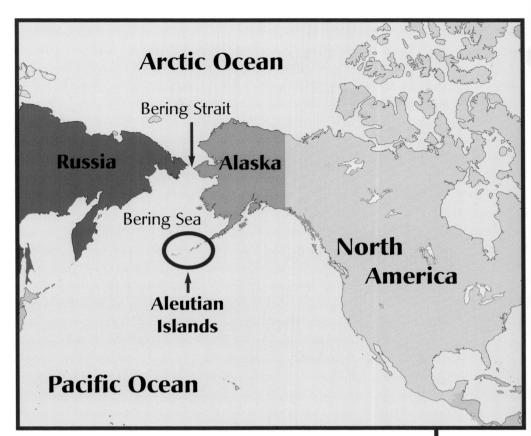

Arctic Ocean

Bering Strait

Russia

Alaska

Bering Sea

North America

Aleutian Islands

Pacific Ocean

By the late 1600s, Spain and England had colonies in North America. The Russians started to set up colonies in what is now Alaska.

An explorer drew this map in the 1700s. It shows the strait between Russia and Alaska. It also shows a picture of the seals that lived in the waters of the strait.

5

In 1741, Vitus Bering *(VY-tuhs BER-ihng)* and Aleksei Chirikov *(ah-lehk-SAY CHIHR-yuh-kuhf)* sailed at the same time but on different ships to explore the strait. A storm separated the two ships. Bering's ship landed on an island, where he died.

Chirikov sailed on to discover several of the Aleutian *(uh-LOO-shuhn)* Islands and the mainland of Alaska. He returned to Russia after his discovery. Fur hunters soon began to set up small settlements in Alaska and on the islands around it.

The Fact Box

The Bering Strait, the Bering Sea, and Bering Island were all named in honor of Vitus Bering.

Bering's ship, the St. Peter, *hit an island in early November 1741.*

Settling Alaska

In 1783, Grigory Ivanovich Shelikhov
*(grih-GO-ree ih-VAN-oh-vich SHE-lih-
kuhf)* was sent to Alaska by Catherine
the Great, ruler of Russia. Shelikhov
helped build the first lasting Russian
settlement there in 1784. The settlement
was on Kodiak *(KOH-dee-ak)* Island.

*The Kodiak Island settlement had houses,
barns, a blacksmith shop, and a carpenter
shop. This picture shows what Kodiak
Island looked like in the early 1900s.*

Grigory Shelikhov brought 192 men and one woman, his wife, Natasha, to Kodiak Island.

The Fact Box

By the early 1800s, Russian hunters were sending about 62,000 furs a year back to Russia.

Russian Trading

In 1799, the Russian-American Trading Company was formed. Czar Paul I of Russia gave the company the power to explore, trade, and begin settlements in North America.

From 1799 to 1818, Alexandr Baranov ran the Russian-American Trading Company's settlements in Alaska.

In 1806, the Russian-American Trading Company was allowed to have its own flag.

11

Fort Ross

In 1812, Ivan Kuskov *(KUHS-kuhf)* was sent to the land that was to become California. His job was to set up a Russian colony. Kuskov helped build Fort Ross in an area north of San Francisco.

Ivan Kuskov's house

Kuskov enjoyed gardening when he wasn't working. He grew beets and cabbage for the settlers in Fort Ross and Alaska.

Fort Ross served as a trading post. It had houses for workers, a store house, and a small church. People hunted, farmed, and raised cattle to keep the colony going. This picture taken in 1865 is the earliest known photo of Fort Ross.

About 225 people lived at the Fort Ross settlement. Of those, about 100 were Russians. The others were Native Alaskans.

Blockhouse

14

Most of the buildings at Fort Ross were made from redwood trees. The fort had two blockhouses with cannons in them. The cannons were used to guard the settlement.

By 1820, life at Fort Ross had changed. There were fewer otters and seals to catch because they had been hunted for so long.

Many Americans were also moving into the area. Russia was worried that the Americans would take its land.

Since Fort Ross was so close to the water, settlers started a shipbuilding business.

The End of Russia's Colonies

In 1841, the Russian-American Trading Company sold Fort Ross to John Sutter, who lived in California.

On January 1, 1842, one hundred colonists left Fort Ross for a Russian settlement closer to Alaska.

Today, Fort Ross is a California state park.

John Sutter owned the land that would become Sacramento. Gold was discovered on his land in 1848. This discovery was the beginning of the California Gold Rush.

Russia still had settlements on its land in Alaska. However, England owned a lot of land around Alaska. Russia thought that the English would soon want to take Alaska for its own. In 1867, Russia sold Alaska to the United States.

After about 100 years, the Russians gave up their dream of having settlements in the Americas.

William Seward (sitting), a U.S. government worker, made the deal with Russia to buy Alaska. Many people thought it was a bad deal. They called it "Seward's Folly" or "Seward's Icebox."

TIME LINE _____

1741   Vitus Bering and Aleksei Chirikov claim the Aleutian Islands and Alaska mainland for Russia.

1743   Thirty Russians come to Bering Island to hunt for fur.

1784   Grigory Shelikhov builds the first lasting settlement on Kodiak Island.

1799   The Russian–American Trading Company is formed.

1812   Fort Ross is built.

1841   Fort Ross is sold to John Sutter.

1867   Russia sells Alaska to the United States.

21

Glossary

colony (**kahl**-uh-nee) a faraway land that belongs to or is under the control of a nation

czar (**zahr**) a king of Russia

explorer (ehk-**splor**-uhr) a person who searches for new places

folly (**fahl**-ee) something silly

fort (**fohrt**) a strong building or place that can be guarded easily

settlement (**seht**-l-muhnt) a place where people come to live

settlers (**seht**-luhrz) people who come to stay in a new country or place

strait (**strayt**) a narrow body of water connecting two larger bodies of water

trading post (**trayd**-ihng **pohst**) a place where things are bought, sold, and traded

Resources

Books

Alaska
by Dennis Brindell Fradin
Children's Press (1996)

Katya of Fort Ross
by Clara Stites
Fithian Press (2001)

Web Sites

Due to the changing nature of Internet links, PowerKids
Press has developed an on-line list of Web sites related
to the subjects of this book. This site is updated regularly.
Please use this link to access the list:

http://www.powerkidslinks.com/euca/rca/

Index

Word Count: 428

Note to Librarians, Teachers, and Parents

If reading is a challenge, Reading Power is a solution! Reading Power is perfect for readers who want high-interest subject matter at an accessible reading level. These fact-filled, photo-illustrated books are designed for readers who want straightforward vocabulary, engaging topics, and a manageable reading experience. With clear picture/text correspondence, leveled Reading Power books put the reader in charge. Now readers have the power to get the information they want and the skills they need in a user-friendly format.